THE JOE PASS GUITAR METHOD

Chappell & Co., Inc.

CONTENTS

Scales

Scales and their Basic Chord Forms. In order to give the student some direction and help in developing an individual concept of improvising, it will be necessary for him to gain a full working knowledge of scales, melodic lines, harmonic patterns, and a plan for combining these elements into useful practice patterns. With the exception of the Blues solo and the short pieces which conclude this book, everything is written in eighth- and quarter-notes, making it easier for the student to see and hear the musical line as it develops.

Below are six diagrams which are usually learned by all guitarists when beginning to play in first position, the Intermediate form not included.

All scales are played vertically within each form whose object is to provide a framework in which to function. Once the pattern in each Form is perceived the location of notes and pitches will become automatic and a familiarity with the fingerboard will be achieved. With the Chord Forms acting as points of anchor or reference, the ability to create an improvised scale or melody will be unhampered by the struggle to find the notes.

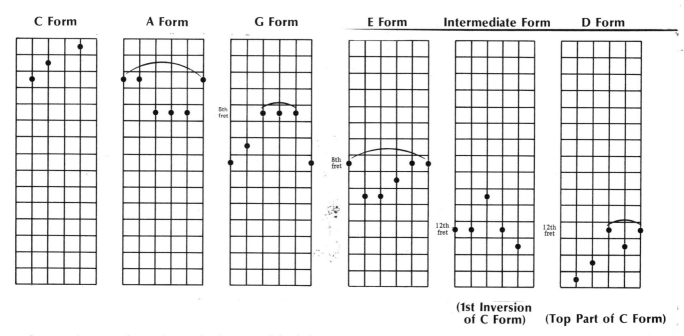

The numbers without circles indicate the fingers of the left hand: **1 2 3 4**
The numbers in circles indicate the strings:

4 | **Major Scales.** The fingerings are intended as suggestions. There are no fixed fingerings and many different possibilities; those which best suit the player's hand should eventually be adopted. For the C Form I always start with my 4th finger on the **A** string. All scales begin on the root C and all are given in the key of C.

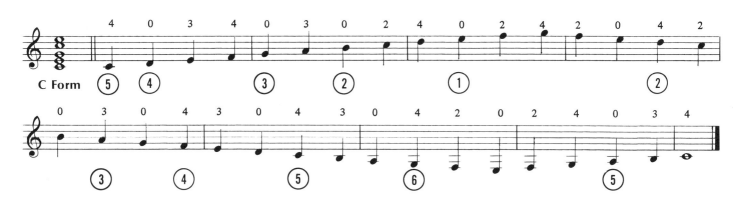

C Form

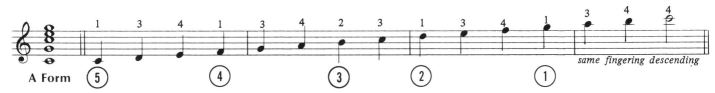

A Form

Alternate fingering: start with the 2nd finger on the **A** string: 2-4 on **A,** 1-2-4 on **d.**

G Form

Only one fingering is possible: the root C is on the 8th fret.

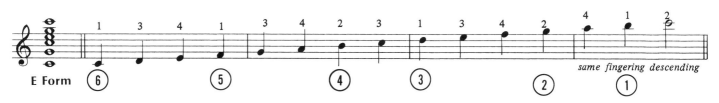

E Form

Alternate fingering: 2-4 on **E,** 1-2-4 on **A,** etc.

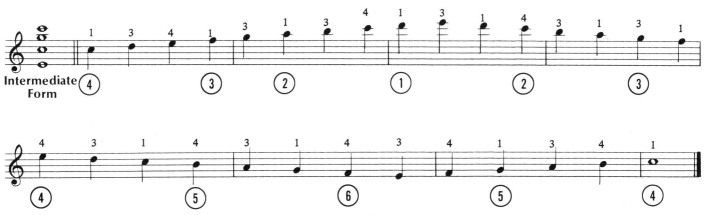

Intermediate Form

The fingering given above is the most practical, especially beginning 1 on **g** (10th fret).

The C and D Forms are related: starting with 4 on **A** (15th fret), it is identical with the C Form in the first position.

It is possible to move up or down a step for a note, so that each Form may encompass about 5 or 6 frets.

As familiarity with the fingerboard develops, the student will discover choices to be made regarding the same note. In the G Form the note B is possible on the **d** or **g** strings. It is best to learn to play the scale both ways, subsequently appropriating the one which feels best. (If all possibilities were given, this book would be filled with nothing but numbers.) By mastering all the scales in the A — E — C/D Chord Forms, which are basically similar, the student will have covered the fingerboard quite thoroughly.

Other Scales. While all the Chord Forms are given for the Melodic Minor Scales of C, only the C Form is given for the Natural Minor and Harmonic Minor Scales. These scales should be repeated in all Forms; the fingering is the same as described for the Major Scales. Only the E Form is given for the Altered Dominant 7th Scale, but again, this must also be practiced in all the Chord Forms.

MELODIC MINOR SCALES

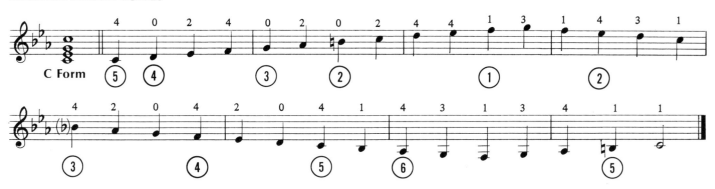

6

NATURAL MINOR SCALE

HARMONIC MINOR SCALE

DOMINANT 7th SCALES

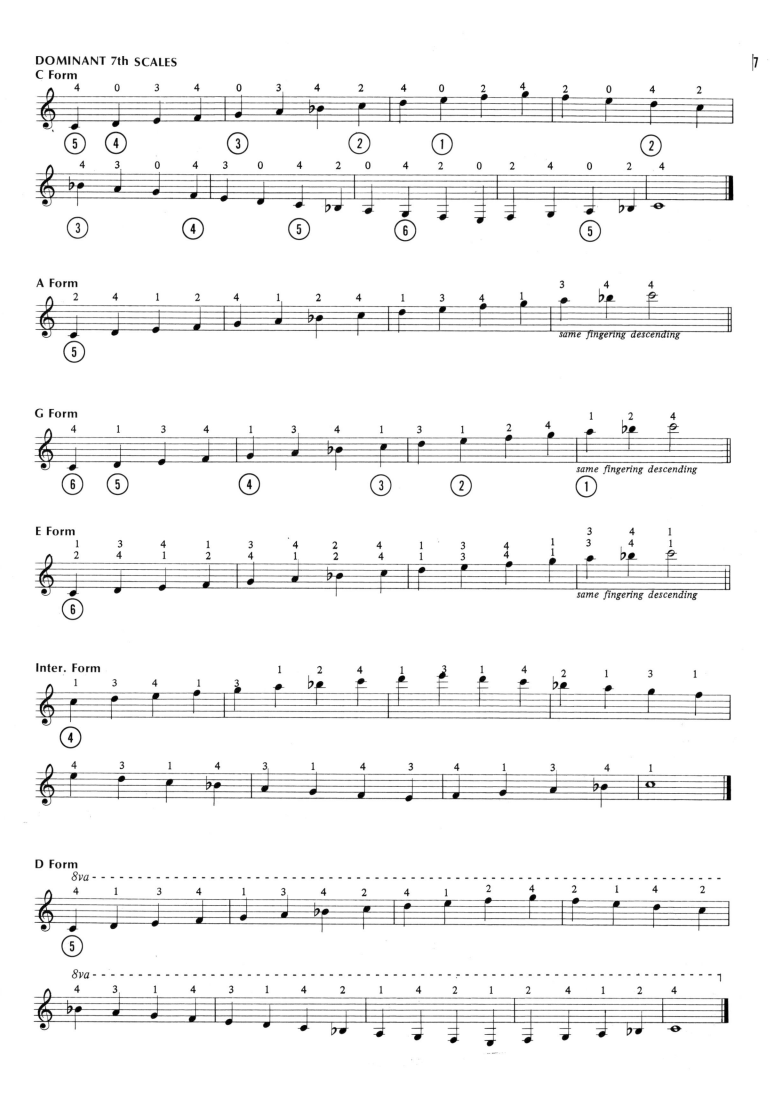

C Form

A Form

same fingering descending

G Form

same fingering descending

E Form

same fingering descending

Inter. Form

D Form

The Augmented, Diminished, and Dominant 7th Scales are influenced by the Dominant 7th Chord. For example, the chord G7 +5 is augmented and can be interpreted linearly by an Augmented Scale. Likewise, G7♭9 is a diminished chord against which a Diminished Scale can be employed. For improvisation the ♭9 and +9 go together. Against almost any Dominant 7th Chord, I will include the ♭9, +9, ♭5, or +5 in my lines, which is the Altered Dominant 7th Scale [See page 10] in most cases but the student is cautioned to use his ears. Applying what he has learned automatically, without considering if it is appropriate, will never lead to any kind of distinguished style.

All scales should be practiced in all Forms either chromatically or in Form order: in chromatic order, play the scales of C in C Form, then D♭ in C Form, D in C Form, etc.; in Form order, play the scales of C in each of the Forms C-A-G-E-Intermediate-D. All scales should extend two octaves, beginning and ending on the root, except for C and Intermediate Forms.

AUGMENTED (Whole Tone) SCALES

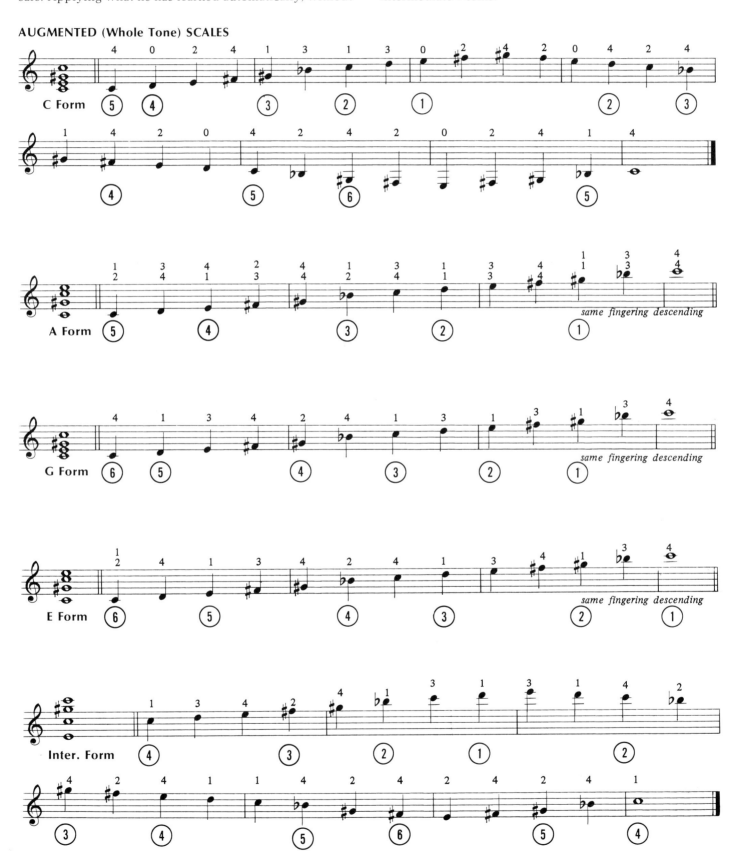

Practice with definition in mind. Each note should be played evenly and clearly and the tempo increased very slowly. This will train the fingers of the left hand to know where all the notes of the fingerboard are located.

DIMINISHED SCALES

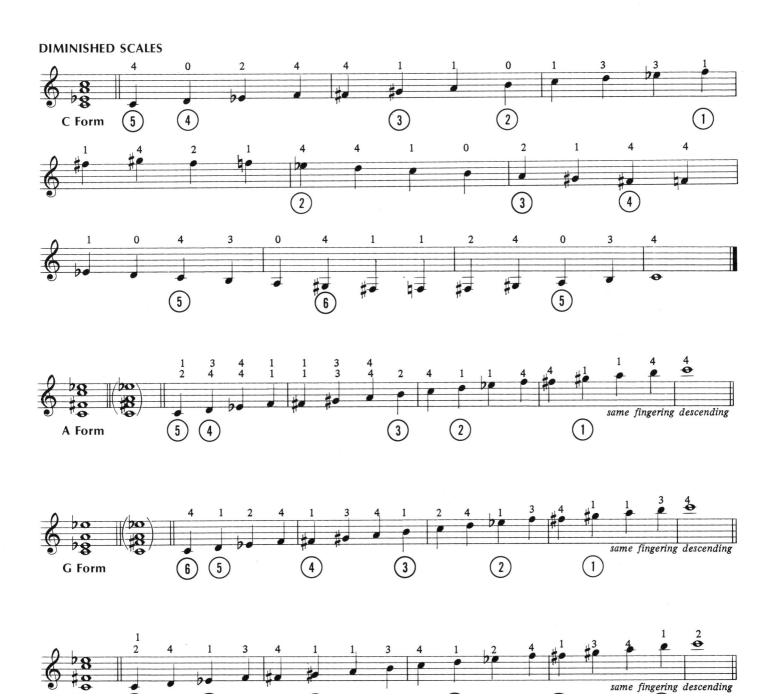

C DOMINANT 7th ALTERED SCALE   E Form

same fingering descending

G DOMINANT 7th ALTERED SCALE   E Form

same fingering descending

Picking. In my own playing I use alternate picking generally. When I shift from string to string, I use down-picking regardless of whether I am shifting to lower or higher strings. Picking is something the student will develop through practice. However, it is essential to be aware of all the ways there are. My habit of alternate picking is peculiar to my style. The student must find his own which will best suit his personal concept.

PICKING EXAMPLE

Practice Patterns

The **Practice Patterns** which follow will aid the student in developing his own ideas. It is recommended that these patterns be practiced in all keys and scales. By inventing his own patterns the guitarist will gain a sense of melodic construction that will be uniquely his own. This will be a great advantage in improvising.

Try taking a chord sequence such as C — A7 — Dmin — G7 — C and constructing an eighth-note exercise over four or eight bars. Then try to extend the chord sequence using

eighth- or sixteenth-notes. While striving to establish continuity and a melodic sense through scales and patterns, always keep in mind that the music must come from the head, not simply from the fingers running up and down the neck. It is important to sing or hum the musical ideas one wants to play while playing them [See page 14].

The following **Practice Patterns** should be practiced in all Chord Forms and keys. The first four examples can be extended at least to eight bars.

C MAJOR EXERCISE

(Ascending and descending within the limits of the Chord Forms)

EXERCISE IN THIRDS   **EXERCISES IN SCALE PATTERNS**

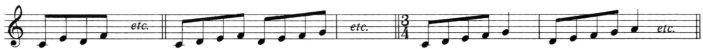

VARIOUS COMBINED PATTERNS

STUDY IN 8th NOTES   A Form

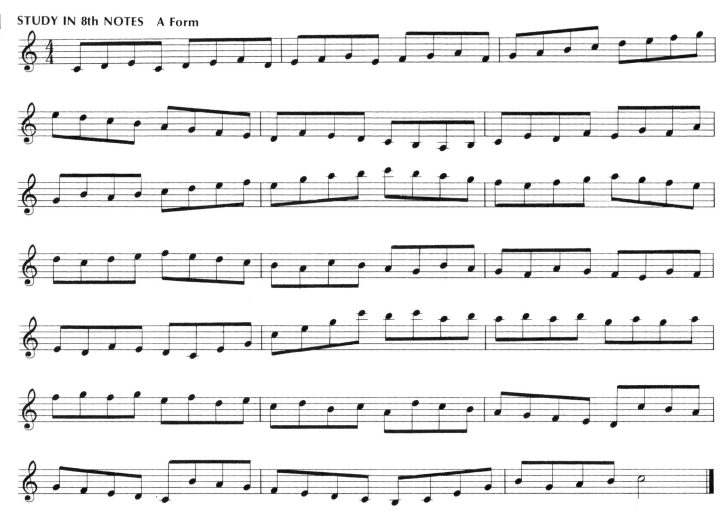

The above study can be played in any of the Chord Forms.
Note the various patterns: thirds, scales, trills, etc.

IMPROVISED PATTERNS   A Form (C Minor)

Whole Tone Scale

DOMINISHED SCALE PATTERN

DOMINANT 7th SCALE PATTERN

EXAMPLE OF FREE IMPROVISATION

The student should try to create some melodic patterns of his own. Also, the underlying chord sequence for this study should be analyzed, remembering that it can be broken down into three simple chord types: Major, Minor, and Dominant 7th (Aug./Dim.).

Chromatic Patterns

The following **Chromatic Patterns** and **Variations** are some which I still practice. The student should make up his own starting with open **E,** then moving up by half-steps to extend the exercise.

Scales Based on Chords

The chords on which these scale lines are based should be played at the beginning and ending of each exercise. In moving from one position (Chord Form) to another, one can shift to any string by using either the first finger or fourth finger to play two notes. This will place the hand on the next Chord Form.

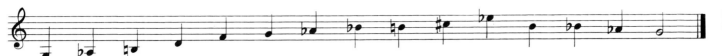

DIMINISHED CHORD LINES or D7 (♭9/+9), F7, A♭7, B7

There are only three Diminished Scales. The five examples are all to be played against Dominant 7th Chords. Find the chords beyond the B7 given.

There are but two Whole Tone Scales. They will fit with all Dominant 7 +5 Chords. Additional Augmented Scale Lines should be developed by the student which will fit Dominant 7th Chords.

C AUGMENTED (whole tone)

C9(13) Dominant Scale Lines with added tones.

C♭5 Dominant Scale Lines with added tones.

Cm(7/6/9) Minor Scale Lines with added tones.

Chord Sequences

The melodic/scale patterns, in the following examples, grow out of the chords at the beginning of each line, which should be apparent when they are played. It may help the student to develop his own ideas by first putting the changes on tape and playing lines against them or having someone else play the changes with the student. These changes should be played out of tempo so that the student can establish a long line and fully realize the potential richness of each chord.

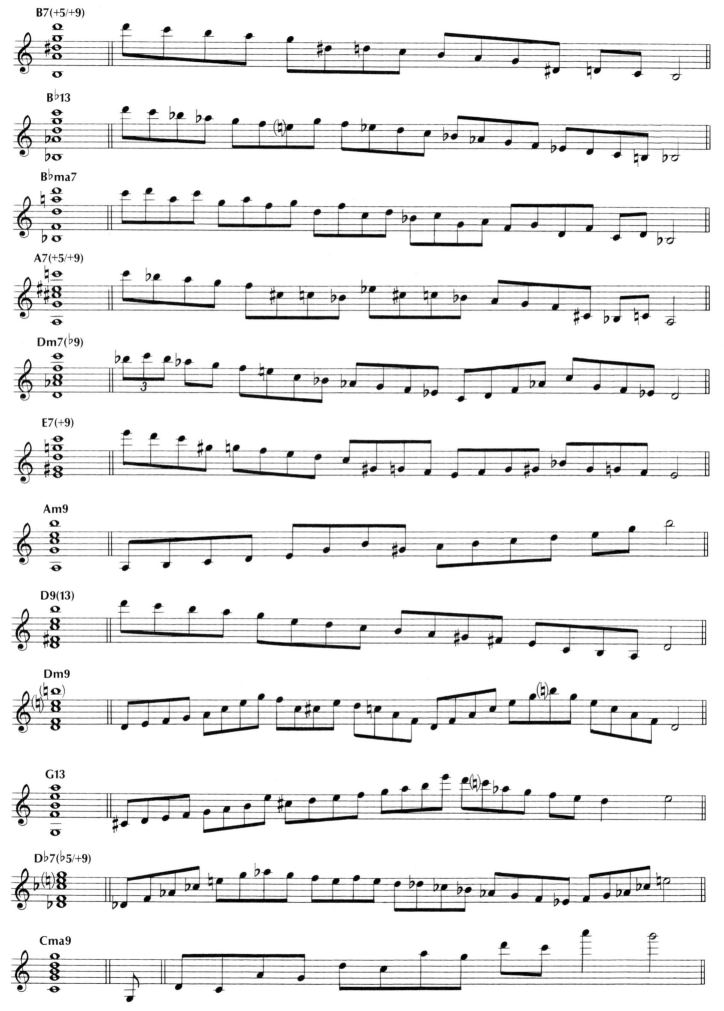

Blues Lines

Though most students know these **Blues Lines,** they will serve as a reminder to those who may have forgotten them.

Pentatonic

Jazz Licks

The **Jazz Licks** will acquaint the student with some of the basic phrasing and germinal ideas. Most are based on the Dominant 7th Chord (C7) since many people seem to need guidance in their exploration of its possibilities, especially in distinguishing it from the major chord. Students are urged to memorize these licks, then try incorporating them into their own improvisations. All the phrases must be played within at least three Chord Forms and transposed into all keys. They should be practiced repeatedly at a medium tempo until the student can sing them and hear them and feel them.

When playing a Dominant 7th Chord or Scale, one Chord Form must be kept in mind. By constantly using and thinking in terms of the Basic Chord Forms and simply flatting the seventh tone, the number of mistakes made in playing on the Dominant will be greatly reduced.

JAZZ LICKS

Phrase Feeling

Joe's Blues

Joe's Blues is based on the blues in the key of G; the chord changes are basically G7 — C7 — D7. These appear in the first twelve bars to indicate the sequence. The following variants may be used in place of G7: G13, G9, G9(6), G7 +9, G7(♭9). D♭9 in the fourth measure can be played in the same way. In bar 8 Bm7 can be replaced by F13/F9/F +9/Fm9. Bm7 can be changed to a Dominant 7th (B7) or B9/B13. The substitutions can be made in the second half of bar 8. E7 can be replaced with E +9/Em9/E13/E9 or B♭9/B♭ +9/B♭m9/B♭13/B♭9. Bar 9 can be altered in much the same way since these chords are interchangeable.

Students must be able to choose freely from the alternatives available not only in chording but also in solo improvisation. In **Joe's Blues** the student should check out each phrase against the chord he thinks is being used.

Joe's Blues

JOE PASS

delay 16 ths

delay triplets

Bass solo

Blues for Nina, Nobs, Alison, and **Grete** are simple melodies used as bases for improvisation. They are recorded on the Montreux Solo Album (Pablo) 1975. Throughout,+9/♭9/13/9(6)/11/+5/♭5 may be substituted for simple Dominants. All changes should be reduced to three- or four-note chords. And for better movement, voicings should lead into one another or have a common tone connecting them. **Nobs** contains several examples of this technique.

Blues for Nina

JOE PASS

Nobs

JOE PASS

EXAMPLE OF CHORD VOICING

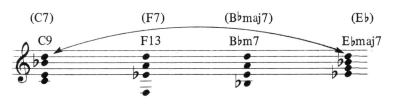

EXAMPLES OF VOICE LEADING

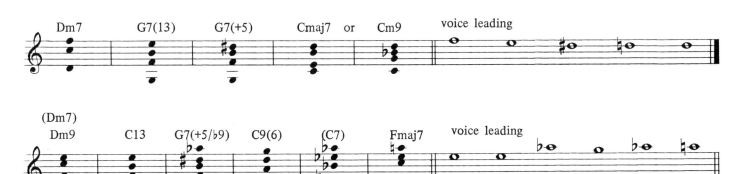

Alison

JOE PASS

EXAMPLE CHANGES FOR IMPROVISING

| Bb7 G13 Cm7 | F7 | D7 G7 | C7 F7 | Bb Bb7 | Eb Edim | 1. Dm7 G7 Cm7 F7 | 2. Cm7 F7 Bb |

Grete

JOE PASS

U.S. $7.95

ISBN 0-7935-2148-3

HL00347734